MORNING GLORY

BE ENCOURAGED!!

MONISHA RODRIGUES

Made with ❤ on the Notion Press Platform
www.notionpress.com

Contents

Contents

Preface

From the Author's Desk...

Hello there! My name is Monisha Rodrigues, a wife to an amazing husband, a mother to two beautiful daughters, a Corporate trainer, and an ICF coach; yet more than anything, a true believer in the power of prayer and a daughter of God, who needs His presence every hour and every day.

Even though I wrote this book, I must admit that I am not flawless and that I require the same grace and courage to go about my day as you do. I still have days when I stumble; I'm still frail, and my faith wavers. As a result, I am completely dependent on Jesus and His assurances and promises; this book is all about experiencing His love and beauty in everything!

As you read and reflect on each chapter, may you experience His presence and be blessed with His peace!

Morning Glory
Preface

Hello there!

The Covid era is where this book's adventure began. The Lord moved me to sit and write down the things that were helping me cope with my emotional upheavals. After COVID, I became quite occupied with my job and advancing in my career. In addition, I had certain health concerns to attend to. I had to cope with my health, a few setbacks, and the loss of my father, which made this time really challenging.

Nevertheless, I got as close to the Lord as I could during my time of prayer, reading the Bible, and meditating on the words I read. The Holy Spirit's soft whispers brought about healing and reconciliation.

Through this book, I hope to inspire and uplift you.   No one has ever had it easy . There is always somethings that trouble us more than others. In the following short writings, each one for one day of the month, I have put in illustrations, examples and events from the Bible and my life too.

You and I both need encouragement. As we work to support one another every day, I pray and hope that this book gives you a new outlook on life and the ability to face its obstacles with a renewed sense of strength from above.

Be blessed !!

Monisha Rodrigues

CrossRoads

Crossroads is the term we use when in confusion or when we are being indecisive. I have been at many crossroads in my life. I have experienced confusion, fear, and doubt, all in a good mix. I have also turned to many people; some have been very helpful, while others have added to my ordeal. This is the time I go into my room, get down on my knees, and ask my God, my counselor, my father in heaven, to whisper His words into my ears. Although the answer may take some time and sometimes may not be what I want to hear, yet He never fails to speak in His still, small voice.

Every time I am at crossroads, I am reminded that I have not walked alone; there has been another who walked that path before me: Jesus walked to the Cross at Calvary. The road not many would want to travel. I am confident that my Lord will accompany me. The road that He walked was never easy, yet it led all mankind to victory—victory over every confusion and dilemma.

Encouragement: Father, remind me that every crossroad is an opportunity to walk with you and to find new paths! When I am confused, I will seek your wisdom in patience. I will draw close to you to hear Your still, small voice guiding me in this world of chaos and distractions.

I will call upon you, and I know that You will answer me. (Jeremiah 33:3) Call unto Me, and I will answer you and show you great and mighty things, which you do not know.

Prayer: Guide me, Lord, to make the right decision; help me, Holy Spirit, as I seek clarity in this current situation. Let me spend more time with you as you guide me.

MORNING GLORY

CHAPTER TWO

Masterpiece

God Never Runs out of Creativity

Do I find it difficult to be different in a crowd? Have I been looked down on because I look different, speak differently, or have different opinions?

I do stick out, yes. I have a different way of thinking, and I don't follow trends. In contrast to people around me, I want to show my originality, my thoughts, and my boundaries. Despite my differences, I want to serve God in all I do, including how I dress, how I speak, and how I treat others—even if it means standing up for what is right when no one else is.

I have learned that once you decide to follow Jesus, you will be looked at differently. Your ways will not anymore be the same as those of the world. You were made for better and bigger things.

My encouragement to you: Recall that God saw fit to create you just the way He did, regardless of what others may say about you. He declared that everything in this world was good when He created it, and He did the same when He created YOU.

If being and appearing different has ever made you feel less than others or less privileged, let the Holy Spirit remind you today that you have been made in the eyes of God the Father; you are fearfully and wonderfully made. (Psalm 139:14). Now rejoice in His love for you and live the life He gave you to glorify Him in all that we do.

Prayer: Thank you, Lord, that I am unique in my own way. Help me not to compare myself with others, but to thank you for all that I am.

CHAPTER THREE

Talitha Koum

What is more heartbreaking than dealing with grief? Jairus, an influential man in the synagogue, had a daughter who was very sick. He had heard of Jesus and went out to get Him, hoping that his daughter would be healed. When Jairus saw Jesus, he fell at Jesus's feet. He asked Jesus to come and lay His hands on his daughter so that she could be well and live. Before Jesus could reach his house, people from Jairus's household came to him and broke the news that his daughter is dead and told him not to bother Jesus anymore. Who were these people from Jairus's household? Maybe those closest to him.

Sometimes, when you pray for what you need—a job, a marriage, a relationship, a kid, or healing—you encounter resistance from inside your own community. You stand firm on your dependence and submission to Jesus, but then it feels like it's over; that's what people have told you.

In this situation, I encourage you, dear friend, to speak the words "KOUM" over that situation, over you. Stand and arise, arise in more faith, arise in expectation, arise knowing

God is doing something new, something impossible in what the world calls to be dead. (Mark 5:41). Jesus is ever so close to you in your deepest moments of pain and defeat. Trust Him to raise every situation that sounds insurmountable. "KOUM!"(Read Mark 5: 35-43)

Reflection: Bring everything you believe is dead, everything you have given up on, and everything you believe will never work out to Jesus today. It could be a circumstance, a person, an occasion, or a dream that

God has placed in your heart. Put it in writing and present it to Jesus.

Allow Jesus to respond to your written plea with the same words that He uttered over Jairus's daughter.

CHAPTER FOUR

Breaking Free

Have you ever felt burdened? Heavy with worry? Yoked? We all have been there! When we are yoked with the worries of this world, our gaze is downward, our strength is gone, we're slowed down in all we do; we are tired and weary. What could be a way to do away with this yoke? With your worries? With your anxiety?

Today, the Lord would exhort us to throw off the yoke and the chains that have imprisoned us. The burden was never intended for you to bear; rather, it was taken on by our Lord Jesus and was relieved by His priceless death on the cross. Give yourselves to Him now.

Bring Him your burdens—physical, financial, emotional, relational, or whatever it may be—big or small, while you sit at His feet. You will find insight, peace, and joy in following His instructions if you sit and pay attention to His quiet, small voice.

My encouragement to you: What causes you to feel exhausted? Give to God right now if you are experiencing worry or anxiety about anything in your life or your present circumstances. He is concerned about you! He has an unending love for you. He promises never to abandon you. (1 Peter 5:7).

Reflection: Bring to Jesus that which is weighing you down. Ask Him for the great exchange, Beauty, for your ashes.

CHAPTER FIVE

Abba Father

I have a Father in heaven. I know He sees me and hears my every cry to Him. He is my Father God. Even when I do not see Him physically, I can feel His presence that strengthens me. He will never let His Daughter walk alone or be lost.

I have to only call unto Him, and He will answer. This is His promise to me, and I know my Father always keeps His promises.

If anyone has to get to His Daughter, they have to go through Him. He will not let any harm come to me if I walk in His way and be in complete obedience, even when I find it difficult, even when it's a lot to give or ask.

Unexpectedly rewarding and surprising me, my heavenly father shocks me. I'm always looking forward to seeing what surprises my father has in store for me each day. He is a kind Father who corrects me with love. He says things that are so full of grace and love, and I want to absorb those traits from Him and become more and more like Him every day.

When I make mistakes, He gently prods me to turn to Him for forgiveness. He never delays in his plans. When the moment is right, he wants me to have the best. Though He is the only one who truly knows me, I nevertheless get frustrated from time to time. He knows what's best for me because He formed me.

My Father in heaven is the one who never gives up on me.

Reflection: Read the Scripture verses mentioned herein. Study each word and meditate on it to be filled with God's Fatherly love. (Jeremiah 33:3) (Jeremiah 31:3) (Mathew 28:20)

CHAPTER SIX

Refiners Fire

Fire represents heat, ash, and burns; it also represents purification and testing of character. Testing through fire is something no one enjoys. These are the final few things we would never want to pray to God for. Let me take you to the Book of Daniel. Because of their steadfast devotion to serving God, I can't even begin to comprehend what it would have been like for Shadrach, Meshach, and Abednego to enter that fire, the 3 young lads who were tested for their obedience and devotion to what they believed **(Book of Daniel, Chapter 3).**

"Please, no! This is not what I want!" would be our normal response to such testing. I was listening to the song **Refiners Fire by Brian Doerksen,** and as always, it brought about a different understanding of the fire in our daily walk with God.

The lyricist talks of being pure like gold and silver and being in the process of purification. Eliminating impurities would be necessary in order to convey the message that something is wrong and needs to be addressed; it could be a habit, a pattern, or a lifestyle that does not please God! If we ought to serve God, if we desire to be a part of the kingdom work force, we have to get away and burn away all that dross.

I'm working on it too. Whether it is cleaning my speech or my thoughts and actions, whatever it takes to go ahead and serve. As Isaiah admitted in **Isaiah 6:5,** "I am a man of unclean lips "who had to be then purified by burning coals of fire to be set apart.

Each one will go through fire to be tested and tried; each one's fire will be different, and the intensity will be different as well. Being in the fire is never an enjoyable place. Paul the apostle went through fire more than once, yet he never gave up and said very encouragingly to all in **Philippians 3:14:** I press on toward the goal to win the prize for which God has called me heavenward in Christ Jesus.

The question we have to ask ourselves is: Are we willing to give up and burn what does not make us holy, different, or set apart? How much do we desire to be faithful laborers?

We must remember that when we accept to do the Father's will, we will go through fire. The good news is that we emerge stronger and better versions of ourselves, ones that are more resilient to the world's things.

Social media exposes us to a wide range of information and entertainment, and it has an impact on the people we work with, live with, and love, and our behaviors, thoughts, and actions towards them. It affects what we think about ourselves too!! It is imperative that we allow God to use the Holy Spirit to purify our hearts so that we are prepared for service in His kingdom.

Reflection: My dear brother/sister, let us today meditate on the song mentiond above and ask God to purify us in His love, to be set apart, ready to do His will.

CHAPTER SEVEN

Spirit Things

Genesis: We see that God created man in Genesis. Let's read this part of scripture together: **Genesis 1:26-27:** Then God said, "Let us make mankind in our image, in our likeness, so that they may rule over the fish in the sea and the birds in the sky, over the livestock and all the wild animals, and over all the creatures that move along the ground." 27 So God created mankind in his own image; in the image of God he created them; male and female he created them. And then we again see in **Genesis 2:7** Then the Lord God formed a man from the dust of the ground and breathed into his nostrils the breath of life, and the man became a living being.

What then does this understanding mean for us? In my opinion, God created us, and He breathed life into us. His spirit in us is how it was meant to be. God created us in His image.

Now consider this: God created us to be spirit-filled, which means that our spirits are in harmony with Him. **Matthew 26:41** says: Keep watch and pray, so that you will not give in to temptation. For the spirit is willing, but the body is weak!" Jesus said.

Our spirits are made stronger than our flesh was meant to be. Yet, sin comes through the desires of the flesh. That is exactly what happened to Eve. The flesh and its desire gave way to sin **(Genesis 3:6).** When the woman saw that the fruit of the tree was good for food, pleasing to the eye, and also desirable for gaining wisdom, she took some and ate it. Our desires grow stronger as we feed them. The question is, what are we doing to feed our spirit, our very soul?

For this reason, it is crucial that we protect our spirit being. Not that God does not want us to enjoy the desires of our heart, but he wants the desires to be aligned with those of our spirit, His desires. I think it's amazing that after creating man in the image of God, God gave him a tangible body so he could tend to the garden and eat the fruits of his labor. He brings Eve to Adam's side to assist him because he recognizes the need for material presence and company. God, our Father, is far too gracious to be indifferent to our needs. In fact, when we read **Psalm 37:4**, it says, Take delight in the Lord, and he will give you the desires of your heart.

What is amazing is He promises us the same glorified bodies when we meet Him in Heaven **(Philippians 3:21)**, who will transform our lowly bodies so that they may be conformed to His glorious body according to the working by which He is able even to subdue all things to Himself.

This lets us know that our bodies won't be physical but rather spiritual. By this, we know that our spiritual bodies will be submitted and will be obedient to our Lord. What a wonderful assurance!

After reading this chapter and tying it all together, I believe we should pray for our bodies to be cleansed of all sins, that we do not give in to fleshly impulses that corrupt the spirit, and that we always and forever remain in contact with God's Spirit, which is life-giving and open to everyone who seeks it out.

CHAPTER EIGHT

Hiding to Healing

Have you ever placed the blame for your actions on someone else? Try to avoid acknowledging your responsibilities by shifting them off. Oh, if the response is "yes," don't worry.

This was common since days of old.   Allow me to transport you back to Eden's garden. Is it familiar to you? In the Garden of Eden, Adam—a man created in God's image—was placed in control of everything. He was allowed to eat everything he wanted, with the exception of the fruit from the Tree of Life. Adam was assigned a single task, which he failed to do. Furthermore, he blamed it on Eve when questioned, while Eve blamed the serpent.

Shifting blame stems from pride, which was the root cause of man's downfall. In reality, it is a refusal to acknowledge our own mistakes. A sense of accountability arises when we acknowledge our mistakes without placing blame. accountability for everything that God has asked us to perform.

We were all made for a purpose and to work with people. Shifting or denying to be responsible for our actions and words simply jeopardizes the very kingdom purpose we were made for. When we accept, we are instantly directed ourselves towards a healing process, towards overcoming the very thing that caused the event, which could be a habit or a sin.

People frequently have a fleeting sense of joy that quickly turns to regret and guilt when they realize they have shifted blame or played someone into it. At this point, the healing process must begin. The method is simple; even if accepting responsibility requires a great deal of bravery, all we need to do is seek the Holy Spirit for His freely provided grace. Get healing for yourselves, live freely and joyfully in the Lord, and never stop celebrating Him!

Reflection: Seek forgiveness from God. It's between you and him. Bringing what you put away to God may be extremely tough for you, but don't be afraid to approach Him. Anyway, He is aware of everything. Allow His peace to heal you so you can live freely.

Verse for Reflection: 2 Chronicles 7:14 clearly states If the people who are called by my name humble themselves and pray and seek my face and turn from their wicked ways, then will I hear from Heaven and will forgive their sins and heal their land. (Reflection)

Leaving UR

When He brings you out of UR...GO! Abraham was a man settled in Ur. He was in the family business, doing well for himself at that time. I get a feeling that he was ambitious and wanted something more in life. He was called of God out of the blue. He was a man of great faith, as we see his immediate dependence and faith in the calling.

Abram to Abraham happened only when he obeyed. When he chose to walk with his family and go to the place God was leading him. Abraham never doubted Gods plan for him and his family . What explicit faith!!

We travel through life, and occasionally we become so at ease that we forget what God has given us through His word or through a prophecy. We grow smug.

I wonder what kept Abraham going. Maybe he wanted more than Ur. He aspired, he desired, and he prayed each day, looking up to heaven, wanting to explore more!! Does that sound like you... and then that day when God speaks to his heart and asks him to leave UR...to move forward in faith.

Even though Ur was a huge, prosperous city that was also crowded with idol worship, God nonetheless chose Abraham from there. Something about this faith-based hero would have been present. His heart was known to God! Dear friend, let me assure you, God is also aware of your heart, your ambitions and every aspiration

Even though you may have lofty goals and dreams today, pay attention to that quiet, small voice and spend time with God to allow Him to guide you. When that occurs, move in faith and leave your UR behind. Will it be simple? No, not at all, but I do believe that God will give you the strength to maintain your faith.

Is it a habit, a behavior, an idol you have created, or a place of complacency that God is asking you to abandon? Nothing is too hard for the Lord, so write down your goals and ambitions and place them at His feet.

If you become near to Him, He will get closer to you. Don't have any second thoughts or doubts! As the Lord states, "My sheep know my voice, and they follow me," so you will know when He calls.

God has a way of changing your name and blessing you with a new one. Abram to Abraham, Simon to Peter: Be ready to have your name changed, from what people have called you to being called redeemed, successful, forgiven, washed, precious one, God's Son/Daughter, His Handiwork, His royal priesthood, and a people set apart.

I leave you with this verse to meditate on: **Matthew 5:16:** Let your light so shine before others, so that they may see your good works and give glory to your father who is in heaven." All glory and honor is to God alone!!

Prayer: Thank you, Father, that you have put dreams and aspirations in my heart. Help me to find a way to accomplish what you desire out of them. Give me the strength to leave my old life and my old ways and make those changes that I need to make to walk in your promises. Give me the strength to walk in freedom and walk confidently in You as you chart my course. Let my eyes be fixed on Jesus, the author and finisher of my faith, as you lead me out of UR to the promised land. Amen

Callings

I enjoy reading the passage in the Bible (Matthew 4) where Christ personally invited Peter and John to follow Him. It simply said, "Follow Me!" They were drawn to Him by these words.

When Jesus called Peter and John, I got curious to learn what were they were thinking. Suddenly, the disciples were called. They were just regular men going about their normal lives.

They only needed one call from the master to follow, which leads me to the question, Were they anticipating being called? Were they fervently seeking the Messiah? Were they ever thinking about preparing to follow the Messiah?

As a child, I grew up in the 80's and 90's when the great revival was on in my country or atleast in my part of town. I had heard of Jesus's second coming. I had heard the statement, "Turn or burn!" What I heard scared me. As a religious teenager at that time, I remember going to bed every night and praying that I didn't want to be in hell but with Jesus in heaven. I wanted to be with Jesus when He came. I would religiously pray this prayer every single night.

At the age of 24, I came to know Jesus as my Lord and Savior. It just took me one call, one gentle nudge to follow Him. Why? Because I knew His peace when I heard His voice. It was different—a feeling, a peace that no other voice ever gave me.

Yes, I was going through difficult times. I felt like I was going around in circles and not moving forward during this very difficult time in my life. I lost my in-laws; I lost my mom; I was confused, angry, and anxious. I questioned the very existence of God.

Here is a scripture that gave me the encouragement, and I am sure it will do the same for you.

Psalm 18:6 In my distress, I called to the LORD; I cried to my God for help. From his temple he heard my voice; my cry came before him, into his ears.

He had heard my cry. He called out to me, I was saved. I was going to be with Jesus forever. I guess the same would have happened with Peter and Andrew; they would have been at the end of their rope, they would have been desperate, and they would have been seeking answers and crying out to the Lord in their alone times!

Encouragement: If that sounds like you, He will come for you. He will never leave you or forsake you. He will leave the ninety-nine and come to seek the one—you!

You are His precious; you are His beloved. Don't give up; hang in there. He sees you, He hears you. Be mindful of His voice and follow Him with all that you have. He is ever faithful to those who call upon Him alone.

Reflection and prayer: Jeremiah 33:3, Psalm 18:6, Psalm 121:1.

CHAPTER ELEVEN

The Advocate

Abraham's pleadings—the religious hero & a true gentleman! Lot, Abraham's nephew, who travelled with him out of UR, made the decision to leave his uncle and take the prosperous land when given the option. Nevertheless, Abraham acted with faith and bargained with God to save Lot when God told him that the land Lot was residing in would be subject to judgment and fire.

Was that a lot of pressure? When we read the book of Genesis, we read about the land Lot inhabited, the land of Sodom and Gomorrah. As you read, you will see in **Genesis 19:15-16:15** With the coming of dawn, the angels urged Lot, saying, "Hurry! Take your wife and your two daughters who are here, or you will be swept away when the city is punished."16 When he hesitated, the men grasped his hand and the hands of his wife and of his two daughters and led them safely out of the city, for the Lord was merciful to them.".

What was Lot thinking, I wonder? Was he still on the fence about leaving Sodom? Was he overly enamored with the people, the atmosphere, or the culture? Hey, don't be judgmental about Lot. We also have a "Lot" in us on certain days.

We still hesitate to leave our questionable behavior, actions, and desires, wanting to keep them close to our hearts even after realizing the terrible results of our acts. To break free from the things we have been surviving on and devouring, we require those divine tugs and nudges.

Let's understand: why did the men grasp Lot even when he hesitated? Was it because of Lot's good value system? When you read about Lot, he was way too far to recognize or have the bone to follow any value system. Nope, it was because of the Covenant between the 3 Visitors and Abraham in **Genesis 18.**

What's in it for me, then? When you miraculously are saved from the danger, calamity, or even saved as one who is a believer in Christ, don't forget to give thanks to those who stood up for you, advocating for you before the Lord. Do remember the person who cared for you, prayed for you, and interceded on your behalf even though you kept acting improperly. It was due to Abraham's persistent entreaties, the hero of righteousness and trust, that Lot was given another chance.

Encouragement: I encourage everyone who is praying for their friends, family, and loved ones to be saved, forgiven, healed, and redeemed to keep praying and seeking the Lord for them. Our God is a God who answers prayer. Every prayer circles around His throne, and in due time it will come to pass.

CHAPTER TWELVE

More Love to More Power

Everybody has an inbuilt urge to love and be loved. Seeking this strong feeling gives us the ability to accomplish more.

I have greater ability to live with purpose and a vision when there is more love in my life. The lyrics of the worship song **"More Love, More Power"** by **(Jude Del Hierro/ Vineyard)** caused me to reflect on the true meaning of this.

As a teenager, I went through a phase where I longed to be loved and appreciated by people around me. Both my family and my friends adore me today. I've found that whenever I receive love—whether it be via words or deeds—it always inspires me to show more love.

I still remember the description of love that my husband and I read out at our nuptials 22 years ago: "Love is patient; love is kind. It does not envy; it does not boast; it is not proud. It does not dishonor others, it is not self-seeking, it is not easily angered, and it keeps no record of wrongs. Love does not delight in evil but rejoices with the truth. It always protects, always trusts, always hopes, and always perseveres. Love never fails. **(1 Corinthians 13: 4-7).**

To have all the above attributes, I need strength, motivation, and love. I'm not just talking about loving each other; I'm also talking about loving yourself, your very self. We should take care of ourselves, our relationships, our thoughts, and our physical and mental well-being. Reduce unneeded stressors and treat yourself with love. One of the ways I am able to love more is first to be filled with the love of God, the true love that is unending and without any strings attached. I cannot give away that which I don't have.

Today I make it a deliberate attempt to seek and soak in the love of God every morning. This book is one of the many things that is a product of how God's love has allowed me to spread love.

I've discovered that I can't show and offer love to anyone—yes, anyone—unless I replenish my cup of love. I've come to the realization that I must learn to love myself and take care of myself if I truly want to change the lives of the individuals I encounter along the way. Seeking strength for our everyday battles, big and small, is a wonderful way of self-care. Continue reading the description of LOVE as my acronym for self-care!

L = Lower your expectations of others and yourself.
O = Overcome your Fears with Faith
V = Value yourself and be encouraged.
E = embrace change and move ahead.

CHAPTER THIRTEEN

Last minutes on Earth, yet Eternity in Heaven.

As we read in **Matthew 27**, we come across Jesus the Messiah and Jesus of Barabbas. When Pilate asked the crowd gathered who they wanted released, they shouted "Barabbas." We read how the crowds wanted Barabbas, the criminal, the rioter over Jesus.

I frequently become upset and wonder how the people could have chosen Barabbas when they were aware of his past while Jesus stood silent and undefended. After a few minutes, I thought, Why only blame the crowd? We are part of that crowd on certain days, aren't we?

Many times during our lives, we chose Barabbas over Jesus. The Barabasses we select cause mental riots that then show up in our actions. The riots of unsatisfied passion and anger, the riots of offense and unforgiveness, the criminal acts of pride, envy, and judgment, and so forth

Despite the several times we have crucified our Lord, we still appear to despise the mob that uttered those words aloud. We refuse to acknowledge that, on certain days, we might be guilty as well. We learn that Jesus rose from the dead on the third day, but we never hear what happened to Barabbas. We know that Jesus readily and willingly forgave all as He died on the cross. That same forgiveness is available to us. Just to add, my mum was in her last moments when she accepted Jesus as her Lord and Saviour. It really does not matter when; it matters if you want to.

I encourage you friend, come to the alter and humble ourselves. Jesus always restores. He forgave the crowd, and He forgave the Sinner who hung next to Him on the cross at Golgotha. The sinner who was crucified acknowledged Jesus and asked Jesus to remember him when He comes in glory. The beautiful part is that Jesus heard and assured him that he (the sinner who hung next to Jesus) would be with Him in Heaven even in the last hours of his life. We can discover the same restoration that the criminal who hung next to Jesus did. It's never too late! Let's humble ourselves and deny ourselves. Let's make an informed decision and follow our Master, Jesus the Messiah, closely.

Reflection & Footnote: (Revelation 1:18) I am the living one. I died, but look—I am alive forever and ever! And I hold the keys of death and the grave.

Waiting in Strength

I dislike waiting. That is my battle, my weakness, and my point of pain. At one point in my life, I waited for more than four or five months for one of my clients to pay me for the services I had provided. I want to share with you what I learned throughout that waiting period, which is why I am telling you this. In order to provide you with some background, I come from a household that never had much money left over after the first week of the month. When it came to financial matters, this always made me feel uneasy, especially when I was waiting to get paid.

It's intriguing to learn how God intends to lead you to a place where you conquer your weaknesses. When you believe and walk in His footsteps, He reverses your past and releases you from its grip, giving you a brand-new present and an amazing future. I firmly believe that we are learning to overcome our weaknesses by waiting. I love the verse in **Isaiah 40:31 that says, "Those that wait upon the Lord will renew their strength. They will soar on wings like eagles. They shall run and not be weary; they shall walk and not be faint."**

It becomes better the more I read it and the more I think about it. I've discovered that waiting quietly and trusting in our Lord is preferable to rushing around and battling things beyond your control. It leaves you feeling exhausted; I experienced the same thing. Every day, I would consider the money to come in. I would question who I should talk to and inquire about the situation. I would be so exhausted by these ideas that I would be unable to focus on my work, the assignments I was given, or my projects. This verse quickly made it clear to me that I needed to wait on the Lord and trust him if I wanted my strength restored.

My Encouragement to you: The only path to success is to run with the Holy Spirit's strength and walk in His timing. He is faithful, so wait for Him to come through. I'll sum up by saying that I'm still waiting, believing, and trusting God with all of His promises for my family and me. Take your waiting to the Lords Throne in pray and watch as your soar in His strength.

CHAPTER FIFTEEN

Unfailing Words

Does God Speak? Has God ever spoken to you, through dreams, visions, prophets, and his word? Are you wondering why it's not yet coming to pass? It could be the season of change, of happenings is not yet here.

On my morning walks, I usually take the time to sit down and look at nature. Today my eyes fell on trees far in the distant. A hue of colors that showed me how the seasons were changing. As the seasons never remain the same, the colour of the trees also changes. Thats how nature was created to be, constantly changing.

Yes, everything and everyone change as days and years go by. I have changed, my friends have changed, my kids have grown, and they have changed too. There have been times I have easily given away my trust to people and their promises only to be disappointed. I have waited for people to fulfill their words spoken to me, and this has caused me to lose my peace and even left me heartbroken. Who can we put our trust in, whose word can we take to heart and believe? It's only the Lord's!!

Our God is an unchanging God. If He has said it, it will happen. Hold on to your faith; God's word will not fall to the ground. His word is too worthy. He is not a man that will lie. He is the same God in the Valley and the same God on the mountaintop. Whether He has given you a word through a person or in your time of worship and devotion, hold on. Have faith and be patient.

Reflection: "The grass withers and the flowers fall, but the word of our God endures forever" (Isaiah 40:8). Write down the promises God has given you over the years and declare them over yourself. Claim it in faith by thanking God for it before it even happens.

CHAPTER SIXTEEN

To be Loved incredibly beyond measure.

I am incredibly loved. "For God so loved the world, that he gave his only begotten Son, that whosoever believeth in him should not perish, but have everlasting life" (John 3:16).   I have no idea how many people would suffer for a friend or loved one. Jesus, however, gave his life for you and me.

I would say, "Why, Lord? What do you want me to learn from your sacrifice? You are aware of my innermost thoughts, my most trivial transgressions, my harbouring anger, my holding of grudges, and the deepest secrets of my heart—thoughts that stem from the core of what it is to be human. But when I come to you, you pardon me; you forgive me.

Sometimes, Lord, it's hard to understand and comprehend the problems of this world, the way people behave, and the things that loved ones say. I want to strike back, and I cry out of frustration and rage. Then, your kind Spirit tells me that I must learn to forgive, and I wonder how I can do that when I am feeling so hurt and upset.

I see the cross, and you show me your nail-pierced hands. You forgave the most heinous sin of men, yet I struggle with unforgiveness and anger toward that which appears small. I hear you cry, "Father, forgive them, for they do not know what they do."

Lord, today I ask you to help me to forgive and let go of my bonds because you loved me unto death. Help me to love like you by dying to myself and nailing my human struggles of the flesh to the cross; a symbol of love, strength, and hope. Let me realize that even when I didn't know you and was a sinner, my voice was in that crowd that shouted "Crucify Him!" You saw me and yet went to the cross simply because you didn't see a sinner; you saw a redeemed son; you saw ME .!! Thank you, Lord, that I can always and forever count on you and never ever be disappointed".

Reflection: What is the one thing I wish to affix to that cross today? List all the people I've been harmed by, and then decide to forgive them. Take your time; it might require more bravery. Ask the Lord to calm you and give you His strength and grace; He will always provide it.

CHAPTER SEVENTEEN

Faith in a GPS world.

I enjoy driving since it helps me de-stress, but I always check my GPS and follow my route, paying particular attention to any obstacles, traffic jams, or waiting times. There have been times when I've looked at the map and felt more worn out than usual.

Evidently, we have been granted the privilege of being aware of every development at every stage. We are able to travel and wait for someone to arrive at home because of the GPS that is available. We can track almost anything, anyplace, whether it's food from a cloud kitchen or a parcel that arrives from an internet shopping site. The need to be in charge has made our anxiety levels spike.

How then are we to have faith for that which we don't see, but pray and seek guidance? It wouldn't be accurate to claim that we weren't anxious prior to smartphones, but our only choice was to wait for things to calm down. Today, however, our ability to wait declines! So where do we put our trust? How do we wait?

According to the **Psalmist (Psalm 119:105)**, "Your word is a light on my path, a lamp for my feet." Another Scripture states, "We walk by faith, not by sight **(2 Corinthians 5:7)**. Though it was written 2000 years ago, God understood our need to be aware of what is going on in order to maintain control. He is all knowing; He would have even anticipated that we would likely have smartphones to monitor everything else in our environment. I love the Word because it brings revelation in this day and age.

For all of us, myself included, let's learn to live by faith in a GPS world when we feel the need to know everything. By faith, let's walk in God's Provided Security (GPS), because He loves us, knowing Father God has everything worked out for us.

Reflection: Are you worried about something? Is waiting becoming difficult? Hold on to your faith because faith in God unlocks doors that no man can shut. Have faith that God is working behind the scenes; if you do not see it happening, it does not imply that it is passive. God is making things easier for you; you will get there.

Prayer: May God grant me the assurance I need to pursue the things I have prayed for but have not yet received.

CHAPTER EIGHTEEN

Feels like being Crucified

I'll begin with a query. What leads me to believe that I won't suffer the same fate as Jesus? How am I currently being crucified? I question why my beliefs are causing me to be treated differently. Why do people dislike me when I speak up for what's right? Why do people criticize me for the decisions I've made in life?

I have faced heartache, betrayal, and loss of friendships because of what I choose to believe, yet I encourage you in the words of Paul from **2 Corinthians 8:** "We are hard pressed on every side, but not crushed; perplexed, but not in despair; persecuted, but not abandoned; struck down, but not destroyed'.

So where are the places that I have been crucified?? My workplace, my family, my social circle, and, on days, even in my church. We are more so judged, misunderstood, tagged, and labeled by people closest to us and in places we least expect. I have been let down by my dearest ones, those who I have given my trust in totality, those who I have shared years of fellowship and love with. I have learned to turn my eyes from people to the Lord, who is the same yesterday, today, and tomorrow.

However, keep in mind that this is also for us to be conscious of and vigilant about not crucifying others, just as much as it is for others. According to the Bible, we will be judged on the same standard as how we evaluate others. I pray that the Bible will be a light to our feet and that we will never be in a situation where I hide away from God for what I have done or for the way I have treated others. Retracing the life of our beloved Lord Jesus, who was crucified by the intellectuals, Sadducees, and Pharisees of His era—the same individuals from the temple and the Sanhedrin. Yes, you read right: crucifixion, separation, and isolation can happen amongst and within your best people in the best places.

It occurred back then, and it does so now! I would like to share a verse that gave me consolation in times of weakness, hurt, & pain from **Isaiah 42:3**: "A bruised reed he will not break, and a smoldering wick he will not snuff out. In faithfulness he will bring forth   justice." This was my healing verse, which kept me strong and gave me hope to carry on. I pray and hope it strengthens you and brings you peace.

Reflection: Dear Lord, help me not to judge others but trust that you are God and always will be, no matter what. When I am being judged and labelled for following you, let me know that my reward is in heaven, and earth is a passing abode.

Let me please you and you alone and no one else in all I think, say, and do. No man before you! You are the Alpha and the Omega! I love you because you first loved me. Holy Spirit from on high, strengthen me and comfort me when I feel crucified and left alone. Let me know that I have you with me and you will never leave me, a bruised reed you will not break. Thank you for your everlasting love. He who trusts in You, Lord, will never be put to shame. Amen.

CHAPTER NINETEEN

Leave the Tomb Behind.

Life is all about opportunities. If we aren't prudent to recognize it, it slips away. Rarely a few receive a second opportunity. This chapter brings us insight about a man who was given a great second chance. It is about Lazarus rising and getting a second chance at life. After his death, Lazarus was buried. For him, everything was over, and there was no turning back. I am sure he would have been excited to know that life was happening again for him. The question is, can I get a second chance at living life?

However, Jesus called out Lazarus from the tomb. To what did He specifically call Lazarus? Was there something more, was it just another opportunity to exist or to live for Gods glory? I often wonder did Lazarus have any regrets that he brought forth in his new resurrected life or did he walk free? Did he carry grave pebbles and grave clothes or did he leave all inside the Tomb?

The Lord did really call me from my tomb, my dark place , where hope failed to exist. I was covered in grave clothing, heavy unwanted burdens and hurts of the past and I had fallen asleep immune to my sins when He called me.I heard His voice, woke up and walked. He removed the burial garments, gave me another chance at life, and hugged me with His Love. Yet, I wonder, though, if I have truly left the tomb.

There are times I have realized that I have a few tomb pebbles that I carry with me. I may have come out of the tomb, but has the tomb come out of me? Do I even realize that if He had not called my name, I would still be rotting and smelling inside that big black hole, believing that was all I had in life?

When Jesus calls me, even today I have to come to understand that the tomb no longer has me. I am called. I cannot come out of the tomb and yet carry a dead mentality, full of despair and sorrow, anxious and worried, but that of joy, hope, and peace. Is it easy? Not at all. We tend to go back to visit the tomb on days, but yet in our weakness, He is our strength.

I cannot walk dead yet coming out of the tomb; that would just make me a walking dead. When I hear His voice and come out, I will run, walk, and dance for joy; joy that is contagious to all. Nothing has changed for Jesus ever since He raised Lazarus; He is the same yesterday, today, and tomorrow. He still weeps for us; He still comes deeply moved to where we lie dead in our sin; He still prays to the Father for us that through us, as we come out of the grave, people will believe in Him and desire His friendship and love, which is everlasting.

As an encouragement, dear one, when Jesus calls you out of the tomb, remember that someone is looking at you walk out that tomb and is believing to meet with God. Walk out of the tomb free, hopeful, blessed, and as a testimony to Christ.

CHAPTER TWENTY

Being in His Presence

I will start with a verse from the Bible , Numbers 9:17-23 The Message (MSG)When the Cloud lifted above the Tent, the People of Israel marched out; and when the Cloud descended the people camped. The People of Israel marched at GOD's command and they camped at his command. As long as the Cloud was over The Dwelling, they camped.

I now realized the true meaning of this. I have consistently prayed for God's presence to lead me. I have sought the Lord on occasion, but I haven't always taken the time to obey Him. Despite His assurance that He is the Way, I have chosen to go my own way.

I seek God today, and He responds to me faithfully. If you are looking for the Lord's direction in your career, relationships, family, finances, and all of your decisions—including your ministry at church—I invite you to look at this text today.

If God has put you in a place and His presence has been with you and is with you , His Gory as in the cloud is upon, Be still, Stay there , don't move... When the time comes for the cloud to move , pack up and go . The Israelites did this in the dessert , so can we .

I'm going to wait for the Lord to accompany me, for him to move ahead of me like the cloud and the fire pillar. Because my provision, joy, sustenance, and assurance are all under His glorious umbrella. Be patient and wait; the Lord has you covered, both now and in the future.

Prayer : God as I sit in your presence , shadow me in your cloud of peace . Let me know that in your presence is where I belong. Your cloud keeps me cool even in a sun scorched land . Lead me by night with Pillar of fire , burning down the obstacles as in walk in your obedience and lighting up my way . Be my guide my Master , My Good Shepherd, now and forever !!

CHAPTER TWENTY-ONE

Faith is the Key.

We all have days like this one; on some, I've felt emotionally depressed, and on other days, anxiety has really taken over and I've been overcome by fear. It takes just one sudden thought from nowhere, and then I go spirally down a hole of negativity. In such moments, I have to assess my faith quotient and determine what's wrong. Where did all that self-assurance disappear?

The self-worth and confidence I had been feeling all this time vanished in an instant! My faith faltered. It's not that faith will last forever just because you have it for a day. We need to strengthen our faith. It's similar to building muscle. *(Psalm 56:3) says In times of fear, I will put my trust in the Lord and offer Him all of my strength and faith.* Having trust makes my path clear and gives me strenght.

It's a light to my path, as I am able to see the possibilities my Heavenly Father is capable of and will do it in time to come. And for whatever reason I don't see it happening, faith will have to be the pillar of support and consolation that will comfort me to know that God wanted the best for me. I have in faith thanked Him in prayer, I have in faith bought things knowing that If God said it, it will happen. I remember buying my first carry on bag in faith with a desire to travel and God has answered my prayer and act of faith.

Nevertheless, sometimes I have to accept and believe in things that never happen because God's ways are different from mine, and His thoughts are different from mine (Isaiah 55:8-9) He is far more powerful than we are; we can only comprehend that much with our limited human minds, unlike Him. *Proverbs 3:5–6 says Don't rely on your own understanding, but put all of your faith in the Lord;* He will fulfill our needs in His time, and frequently not in the ways we expect. The Lord has always provided for me and satisfied me in ways I never would have thought possible. He has ben faithful and expects the same measure of us being faithful to HIm and trusting His timing .

My Encouragement to you is to be prepared to be amazed if you have prayed and praised God for anything. He will provide for your needs, and it might even happen in a very different and special way since that is how our God operates. Use the oil of faith every day to illuminate your way when doubts and fear arise. Refreshment comes from spending time with your heavenly Father, reading His word, and worshiping the Lord. What are you praying for today and hoping to happen in Faith? Go and perform small acts of faith and see how you mustard size faith will be key for bigger blessings & testimonies in your life .

CHAPTER TWENTY-TWO

Job: A man of Prayer.

Job, the man who got not only God's attention but Satan's too. Job had everything he ever needed money, land, livestock and a big family. God had blessed him abundantly. In addition to being wealthy, Job was a devout guy. Yeah.. Thats Job.

He had a deep affection for God. According to the book of Job, despite his wife's provocation, he refused to curse God even after losing everything, becoming ill, and experiencing agony. Job lost everything and yet he decided to stand firm in God. As a parent, there is one verse in the Book of Job that mentions Job regularly prayed and interceded with God for the forgiveness of his children's sins.

I am a parent of 2 daughters, and I know the anxiety that I go through on days just thinking about them being out in the world. Being an intercessor for our children is the most crucial thing a parent can do. We never know what challenges our children, siblings, or loved ones will experience or conquer in this life. The language they use, the stuff they watch on television, their ideas, and the company of people they decide to maintain.

Prayer is a powerful tool. It's not the tool of last resort. It's you standing in the gap for those you love and care for; it's asking God to turn His eyes and change the hearts of those that really mean a lot to you. I have had the opportunity to pray for my friends, my cousins, and even my colleagues at work. I have used prayer as a weapon to shield me when I feel endangered, and I have used prayer in times of my desperation.

As we live and journey through life together, its good to pray and ask God for His grace and mercy for our loved ones. Yes, we also require it!

To deal with every changing stage of life, to carry our cross of troubles, challenges, and weariness every day, and to bring it to the feet of the Savior in total surrender. We need our loved ones, friends, and kids to pray for us constantly. God adores a church, a group of friends, a fellowship, and most importantly, a family that prays for one another. Today, let's make it a practice to bring each of our own to prayer. Have you prayed for those you love today?

Reflection: Let us name our family members and our friends and pray that God will forgive any sin that has been done consciously or unconsciously. Bring your transgressions too before the Lord today. If you have to forgive anyone, do it now before the Lord. Our Lord is faithful; He is slow to anger and abounding in love.

CHAPTER TWENTY-THREE

Unrestrained Love.

Jesus loves me without restraint, recklessly! He adores me! Who is capable of love like His? He is always there, and the love He gives me is unmatched in the world!

I become inspired when I hear these phrases as I sit in worship with the song Reckless Love by Cory Asbury . It demonstrates to me that even in my sin, God still loved me and yearned for me to turn to Him. I know that I don't always have to strive to be the best for God. He can take even the little things that I do and use them for His glory. As a working mom, I feel so good when I come home and I am greeted by a hug from my children. There are times my kids will make me a cup of tea with biscuits. This leaves me wondering if we as parents feel blessed with these small acts, how much would God our Father love us for the things we do in love for Him?

His love is never-ending; the further I run, the more He keeps pursuing me with His love, showing me through various signs that He loves me. Yes, this is me when I need love, trying to run to find it, running after it; little do I know that I have to only stand still in His presence, and He will shower that love on me. He has always loved me. He fights my battle even when I don't know He is.

His love gave me my sense of value, yet sometimes I question myself and minimize his affection for me. I ask myself, what have I done to earn this unfathomable affection? And why this immense love for me , for God is love. I am confident that God will fight my battles, clear my name, and set a table in front of my adversaries today. As my counsellor and champion, He will raise my head. His words are like a beacon that illuminates my path. He still waits for me, the one out of 99, even though He has many people in His affection.

Reflection: If you're feeling unloved today, keep in mind that God's love is still after you. Give up running and surrender to him; his love for you is eternal. Recognize that He is God and remain still in Him. Enter His Presence.

Read & Meditate : Mathew 18 : 12; Luke 15: 3

CHAPTER TWENTY-FOUR

Praise Him.

Our God loves when we worship him. He loves when we Lift him up on our praises . I always wondered why would God want so much Praise and Worship ? Why even in our most difficult days He wants us to Praise and worship Him? How could I do that ?

The Holy Spirit spoke to my heart one day when I was lying down on my bed and answered my question. When we worship, we exalt the name of our Lord Jesus, give him thanks, and declare His greatness. Over all of our concerns, difficulties, anxiety, pains, and illnesses, we invoke His divine might. We openly acknowledge that He is the author and finisher of our faith and that He has complete control over everything!

Now, I want you to take another look at what you read. Do those declarations of praise inspire you even as you utter them? This is the strength of worship and praise! In addition to blessing God's heart, it helps you rise above your current circumstances by reassuring you that He is in complete control, on the throne, and always on time.

Thereby we know, it is evident why Paul and Silas worshipped in the prison. You can be imprisoned by a lot of things today, including your own pessimistic ideas, the things that people say about you, addictions, and personal problems and illnesses.

This is my encouragement to you, You will be blessed, uplifted, and encouraged as you begin to praise and adore God and tell Him what He means to you. Even while your troubles might not go away, you will

undoubtedly get the strength to deal with them. Remember dear friend Praise is our strength in our weakness, and that His grace is sufficient for us.

CHAPTER TWENTY-FIVE

4 in the Fire.

My journey has thrown a lot of curveballs at me. It has caught me unaware and has challenged everything in me. I have been let down by my very own and have been hurt by those who i have given my total trust . I have felt completely defeated; even more felt alone and weak.

A couple of days back, the worship song Another One in the Fire kept ringing in my head; the words and the tune kept coming back. I remembered the passage where Shadrach, Meshach, and Abednego were thrown in the fiery furnace for their unshakable commitment to God, and came out unscathed with not even the smell of smoke on them.

What the Spirit revealed to me during my time of worship and meditation that day amazed me; therefore, I'm sharing it with you to uplift you as it uplifted me.

If you are going through a fiery trial, you feel alone and defeated; you are on the verge of losing all hope; remember the 4 people in the fire! Now if you are wondering, I don't have anyone else but me, so how come 4 in the fire? Here it comes!! We believe in the triune God! Father Son and the Holy Spirit, when you are in that fire, the Triune God will stand with you. Now doesn't that make 4 in all?

I encourage you, my dear brother and sister, in Christ Jesus. You are not alone; you have the support of Father God, Jesus the Christ, and the Holy Spirit. Allow them to make a way in your trials. Invite them in so that they can stand with you and strengthen you, bless you, have favor, and deliver you from the furnace that you are in so that you can come out, unscathed and stronger than before, even without the smell of smoke.

Prayer & Reflection: : Lord, I invite you today to be with me in this time of trials and battles that I am going through. (Speak to God about what is troubling you). If you have a burden for someone, pray for them too. I ask you to be with me, be my strength, my support, and my Savior in his time. Even as I got through with it, help me to focus on your strength in my weakness so that I may come out stronger, more in peace, and feeling more loved by you. Amen

CHAPTER TWENTY-SIX

Bowl of Stew

I come across a lot of decisions that I have to make in my journey, some very difficult, some easier than the others. I have choices that challenge my ethics, principles, and beliefs sometimes. So the question is, What is my bowl of stew? What am I ready to give up for it? You may be wondering, What is this Bowl of Stew analogy?? The bowls in my life are being anxious, lacking faith, peer pressure, temptations, and many more. Yes, I have quite a few bowls that I need to be mindful of. The good news is, I have a choice!

I adore Esau and Jacob's story. Because of his extreme hunger, Esau would rather have a bowl of stew than his entire birthright. If only he had been patient and realized what he was letting go of **(Genesis 29:29-34)**. Yes, it was said that the younger will rule the older, but yet again, just taking back from that chapter in the Bible.

It causes me to reflect on the decisions I make. It makes me question how many times I've caved in to various stew bowls. Esau's bowl was filled with food because of his raging appetite. What am I hungry for? What does my bowl consist of?

Giving up our birthright, our blessings, our Favor for things that are worldly and carnal is convenient. We sacrifice our happiness and tranquillity for something that could be replaced at any time. Each of us has a bowl, which may vary in size, have been handed down through the generations, or we may have chosen to keep it in order to fit in. Let's choose to set aside our bowls today and set aside our fleshly desires, as Paul so eloquently states in **Galatians 5:17–21 (see Scripture).**

Rather, let us exalt our Lord Jesus Christ by means of Holy Communion, the cup He voluntarily drank, and the body that was broken to atone for both your and mine sins. Set down the bowls in exchange for the cup of life through Jesus, Our Lord and Savior, and spend some time today in holy communion with a loved one or even by yourself.

Our God is gracious to us to take away our every sin and remember it no more. He is the God of second chances. You were bought with a great price; do not let a bowl of fleshly desires overtake the chance to eternal life with Jesus.

Reflection: Meditate on this verse. Galatians 5:17:17 For the flesh desires what is contrary to the Spirit, and the Spirit desires what is contrary to the flesh. They are in conflict with each other, so you are not to do whatever you want.

List down your bowls of stew and bring it to the Lord.

CHAPTER TWENTY-SEVEN

The VIP in You.

A few weeks ago, my daughter experienced a difficult time at school. She was deeply hurt by this rejection. I still recall the conversation we had while driving back home, during which she told me, "Mum, I feel like I'm worthless. I believe that I am a burden on the planet and that I am purposeless. Why I was born is a mystery to me." As I am aware that silence can also be a powerful healer, I was unsure of how to react to this and didn't want to say anything.

Yet, prompted by the Holy Spirit, I was encouraged to say to her, "When you feel underserved, remember God sent His only Son to be crucified, who He loved so dearly for you, so that you would know that you are loved, have joy, and experience His Heavenly assurance on earth. He left the 99 sheep and came for you and rejoiced over you!"

There was still silence in the car as we drove after that, but I knew in my heart that this silence was the Lord replacing His love in her sadness, the beauty for ashes moments that we have in Him.

I want to encourage you today: if you have been belittled, mocked at, not appreciated, and are feeling that no one loves you or you are of very little value, remember the Good Shepherd who cares for you, who rejoices over you with singing; He has your name inscribed in the palm of His hands. He will never leave you nor forsake you. Even though your father and mother may leave you, He will never forget you. Precious one, you are more valuable to Him than rubies. He loves you with an eternal love. You are HIS VIP!!

Reflection: Just as King Hezekiah put forth before the Lord the Scroll, fell face down and surrendered to God the threats and words of defeat; put before the Lord what people have spoken against you, and let God change those words into words that bring healing. Declare what the Lord says about you. (Scripture Reference   Read: 2 Kings : Verse 20:2-6

CHAPTER TWENTY-EIGHT

Finding Wisdom & Gaining Understanding.

The two most sought-after qualities that are more valuable than rubies are wisdom and understanding. I have consistently asked God to grant me knowledge and insight. I offer up this prayer of faith for my family and myself.

This sentence has never made more sense to me than when I read **Job 28:28.** "The fear of the Lord is wisdom, and to shun evil is understanding," he declared to humanity. What a marvelous revelation found in God's word!

Working with individuals from many organizations and industries, I observe their drive for perfection, their desire to advance in their careers, and their insatiable curiosity! Sometimes I wonder if there is wisdom in everything they look for. Does anyone understand? Is it possible to avoid evil and still be faultless in our actions? Do we truly reverently fear the ever-watchful Lord, or do we believe He is passive and unconcerned about our welfare?

Well-being comes from having wisdom and understanding!! In a world where evil lurks at every corner, deceitfully entering our very hearts through what we think, what we see, what we hear, and what we say, can we have the strength to overcome and walk in freedom? Yes, we do. It is a simple way of life: **"FEAR GOD, SHUN EVIL"!**

But, Lord, how can I? You will be successful if you follow this statement in order. You should put God first, fear His name, fear His very being since you were created in His image and likeness, fear losing His love, which has carried you this far, and avoid evil. As long as you love God, there is no chance that you will fall victim to evil. Worship Him, for perfect love casts out all fear!

Reflection: Ask the Lord of Love for knowledge and understanding today, and bring Him your weakness. Make the conscious choice to leave behind anything that is contrary to God's word today. When thoughts, words, and deeds are difficult for you, ask God to show you His presence. Footnotes for the meditation: According to Job 28:28 and Proverbs 9:10, wisdom begins with fear of the Lord.

CHAPTER TWENTY-NINE

Leap of Faith

It was an amazing day! I had gone to a gathering of entrepreneurs for networking. "You must do things with a leap of faith," someone advised me during a conversation. As someone who has spent the last 20 years following Christ, I added right away, "My life has been a leap of faith, and that is what has got me this far!"

My path as a woman, wife, mother, friend, and business owner has taught me a few truths that inspire me to take leaps of faith and live in faith. When you jump, you anticipate covering more ground and moving more quickly. Leaps occur at moments of joy, happiness, and freedom from anxiety, as well as in moments of dread. Think about how you would jump and leap out of the way of an automobile that is speeding toward you in the middle of the road. Leaping is energetic!

Why do I choose to leap in faith? I have learned that faith, hope, belief, and assurance cannot always be found in people. There has to be a stronger and more consistent source. I leap in faith because faith never disappoints and hope never lets you down. Psalm 33:20 quotes: We wait in hope for the Lord; He is our help and our shield. I have my hope built on the Lord; I consider everything else to be sandy foundations. To live life with a leap of faith is a good thing; it is always forward-looking and progressive.

Encouragement: I want to encourage you today to leap like a deer, with all of your strength, in faith in God, and then take care of your obligations. Have faith in it. It can unlock several blessings and favors and open doors that have been closed. I hope you never give up on your goals and dreams. When you succeed, inspire and uplift those who have been on your path, and be a blessing to others.

Reflection: Write down at least ten things you would dare to undertake, soaking them in prayer as you hope to accomplish them.

Not the Red Sea this time.

There are numerous miracles in the Bible; one of my many favourites is the Red Sea parting. Following the dramatic deliverance from Egypt, the Israelites were persecuted by Pharaoh's troops. When they saw the Red Sea in front of them and the army behind them, the Israelites' happiness instantly turned to fear. At that moment, God gives Moses the order to raise his staff, and the Israelites pass over to the other side of the Red Sea on dry land **(Exodus 14:21–29)**.

I have used this miracle as a prayer to help me get through difficult situations or when I am trapped and unable to see a way out. It would be wonderful if all of my obstacles and challenges could be overcome as easily as crossing the Red Sea. How pleasant that would be!

However, I came to the realization that not all waters must be separated after the Lord spoke to my heart one morning. It is necessary to cruise on some of them. The Lord will occasionally lead you through a rough sea in order to transform and guide your paths to the place He wants you to be. We shall never comprehend his heavenly purposes, because his ways are not our ways. Not every storm is meant to destroy; some are meant to reroute your course and strengthen your faith.

When I am on my boat in the stormy seas of life's difficulties and hardships, I remember that Jesus is in complete control of the winds that rage and threaten me. Every wave that slams into my wobbling boat is controlled by him. The voices in my thoughts, the discouragements, the failures, and the storms around me can all be silenced by him, too! Not all seas require division; some must be navigated amidst the tides. Be faith-filled and trust His timing!

My encouragement to You: We believe in a God that walks on water. Keep your eyes on Him; let not any fear destroy your faith and trust in Him. He will never let go of your hand. He will restore you. Just fix your eyes on HIM.

Scripture to Meditate on: Matthew 14:22-33

CHAPTER THIRTY-ONE

Are you still Laughing?

Abraham and Sarah had no children and were much ahead of their time as parents. On a day when neither spouse had high expectations, three men just so happened to pay them a visit. It was boldly predicted by one of them that Sarah will give birth to a son around this time next year. Sarah laughs as she hears this statement from behind the tent. When she was asked a question she did not anticipate, she refused to have laughed **(Genesis 18:11–15)**.

Yes, we laugh! We laugh because we find it funny; we laugh when we are nervous as a defence mechanism; we laugh in sarcasm; and we laugh when we don't believe. I have laughed many times to myself because of the enormity of things that people have told me about my future through prophecy. I have laughed in unbelief, especially when those very said words are taking time to be fulfilled. I may not have smirked or laughed aloud, but I know I have. I hope you can relate to what I mean to say.

God knew Sarah's thoughts, just as he knows ours, and I adore what he says to her and Abraham in verses **13–14**. He continues by saying, "Is anything too hard for the Lord?" in verse 14. When Sarah gave birth to a son, she called him Isaac, which means "he laughs." He was the covenant bearer and the fulfilment of the Lord's promise that took place just as it was told to Sarah and Abraham—from a laugh of skepticism to a laugh of promise fulfilment.

This is the last question I want to ask you. Has the Lord given you a promise that you find unthinkable, unimaginable, or unattainable? Do you believe that your current circumstances—your age, your job, your family, your finances—are well beyond their natural time? Do you continue to laugh at whatever feelings are causing you to doubt yourself? Consider this: "Is there anything that the Lord cannot handle?"

My encouragement to you: The Lord will carry out His word if He has said it. The Lord is able to accomplish far more than we could ever hope or imagine. Give thanks to the Lord and watch with faith as your promise is fulfilled. Soon enough, you will experience your Isaac moment—from the laughter of disbelief and doubt to the laughter of delight, excitement, and triumph in the waiting!

Scripture Verse for Meditation: Isaiah 40:31

Chapter to read Genesis 18:11-15

Be Blessed

Hello again Friend   !!

I hope you had a great time reading and being encouraged by God's Word. It's a great place to be: in total surrender, in worship, in adoration!

I truly believe all things are possible with faith as small as a mustard seed. If you would like to explore more of this journey with Christ Jesus and experience His love, you could invite the Lord to be your mentor, your savior, your lamp in the darkness, by simply surrendering to Him, asking Him for forgiveness, and following His teachings that are full of love & hope. You could simply say, **"Lord Jesus, I bring to you my mistakes, my challenges, and ask you to help me get a brand new start in my life's journey. I invite you today to be my Lord & Saviour from now on and forever. Amen."**

Continue to walk in the leading of the Holy Spirit & seek God in all you do!!

Blessings!!